Travis Talks with God

By Jack H. Thornton
Illustrated by Angela Adams

 THE CHRISTIAN SCIENCE PUBLISHING SOCIETY
BOSTON MASSACHUSETTS, U.S.A.

Travis is a little boy
who is not quite old enough to go to school.
He lives in a red house on a little hill.
From the front porch he can look right out at the ocean.

In winter there is lots of snow on the ground,
and Travis and his friends love to ride on their sleds.

They ride from the top of the hill by the red house.
They ride almost down to the ocean. My, but they go fast!

Sometimes they join the sleds together.
Whoever is to lead the way lies down flat on his sled.
He hooks his toes into the sled behind him.

Travis's friends all do the same thing.
Sometimes there are four children
all coming down the hill together.

Travis even loves to ride on his sled all by himself,
and he has never been afraid to go down the hill.
He knows that divine Love is right there with him
all the time. Divine Love is another name for God.

Divine Love isn't something you see with your eyes.
Love is something you just know or feel happy about.
Love can't be in one place and not in another.
Divine Love is everywhere.

Well, one day it was very cold, and the snow was icy.
The hill was so slippery that the sled went faster
than it had ever gone before. Travis even forgot
that Love was with him, and he became afraid.
Because he was afraid, he didn't turn when he should.
The sled went one way. Travis went the other.
Over and over he rolled.

When he finally stopped rolling he was so covered with snow
that he looked more like a snowman than a little boy.
He got up and tried to brush the snow off.

Then he started to look for his sled.
As he took a step, he felt a pain in his side.
He didn't feel at all well.

Whenever Travis didn't feel well, he would always ask
his mommy or daddy to pray for him.
He had learned that divine Love always hears our prayers for help.
He knew that Love can heal anything.
But as he stood there in the icy snow,
Travis wondered why God had not talked with him.
Why didn't God keep his sled from turning over?
A little tear ran down his cheek. He turned
and slowly walked toward the red house on the hill.

He went straight to his daddy
and told him what had happened.
He told him about his side hurting too.
What do you think his daddy asked him to do?
Well, he asked him to talk to divine Love.
Travis was really surprised to be asked to talk with God.

Travis climbed up in his daddy's lap.
Then his daddy reminded him about
what Mary Baker Eddy says in one of her books.
Mrs. Eddy says that a long time ago
men who loved God talked with Him.
Travis loved God, so this meant he could talk with God, too!
It was really fun to think about it!
His daddy asked him to sit by the fire
and talk with God all by himself.
My, but he felt like a big boy!
He was going to talk with divine Love himself.
He was sure that Love would make him well.

As Travis climbed down from his daddy's lap,
he thought it would be nice to talk with God.
The only trouble was that he didn't know what to say.
He thought and thought.
Soon he remembered that Love is everywhere!
So there just isn't room for anything that isn't happy.
There is no room for anything that isn't good like Love.

Suddenly, without making a sound with his voice,
he asked God a question. He thought,
"God, why didn't You talk to me this afternoon?
Why didn't You keep me from falling off my sled?"
Just then, sitting in front of the bright, crackling fire
Travis remembered that God had talked with him!
It was just before coming down the hill for the last time.
Travis had thought that he should slow down on the curves.
It wasn't wise to go so fast when the hill was icy.

These thoughts had come straight from God!
But Travis hadn't listened.
He hadn't done what God told him to do.
Only last week he had learned the First Commandment.
His Sunday School teacher had read it from the Bible.
He knew it by heart. He said it over to himself.
"Thou shalt have no other gods before me."
Why, this meant he should listen only to good thoughts.
Then, he should do what they say! The fire in the fireplace
had made Travis warm on the outside.
His thoughts had made him warm on the inside.
It was nice to talk with God and listen to Him, too.

Travis felt so happy that he said very softly,
"Thank You, God, for loving me."
And he added, "Thank You for Your niceness."
Can you guess what happened then?
Well, while Travis was talking to God,
the pain in his side went away.
While listening to divine Love, Travis was healed!
He jumped with joy! God had heard him!

He went back to his daddy.
He promised to listen more to God.
He knew that no matter what happened,
he could talk with God right out there in the snow.

And best of all, he could do it all by himself!

Note –

Reading aloud to a child is one of the most treasured of life experiences. The words from a story take on love, warmth, guidance, comfort. And the story of Travis tells of the presence and care of God — which brought the very special help of healing to this little boy. The boy who had this healing is grown up now, and his name isn't really Travis, but it is a true story based on his very own experience.

Care for children is a privilege and a responsibility. Of course they always seem safest in our laps, curled up with a book. But beyond that lap, it is reassuring for children to learn that they are always in the "lap" of God and that the protection of God, divine Love, is forever with them as a healing presence and lifelong blessing.

One book that is mentioned by Travis and his daddy in the story is the Bible, and the other one is called *Science and Health with Key to the Scriptures,* a book about healing, written by Mary Baker Eddy.